I'm Like You, You're Like Me

A Book About Understanding and Appreciating Each Other

by Cindy Gainer
illustrated by Miki Sakamoto

free spirit
PUBLISHING®

Library of Congress Cataloging-in-Publication Data
Gainer, Cindy.
I'm like you, you're like me : a book about understanding and appreciating each other / by Cindy Gainer ; illustrated by Miki Sakamoto.
p. cm.
Earlier ed. published as: I'm like you, you're like me : a child's book about understanding and celebrating each other. 1998.
ISBN 978-1-57542-383-8
1. Individual differences in children—Juvenile literature. 2. Similarity (Psychology)—Juvenile literature. 3. Interpersonal relations in children—Juvenile literature. I. Sakamoto, Miki. II. Title.
BF723.I56G35 2011
158.2—dc22

2011011887

ISBN: 978-1-57542-383-8

Reading Level Grade 1; Interest Level Ages 3 to 8;
Fountas & Pinnell Guided Reading Level I

Cover and interior design by Tasha Kenyon

10 9 8 7 6
Printed in China
R18860716

Free Spirit Publishing Inc.
6325 Sandburg Road, Suite 100
Minneapolis, MN 55427-3674
(612) 338-2068
help4kids@freespirit.com
www.freespirit.com

1604

To Bill and August
with love, always.

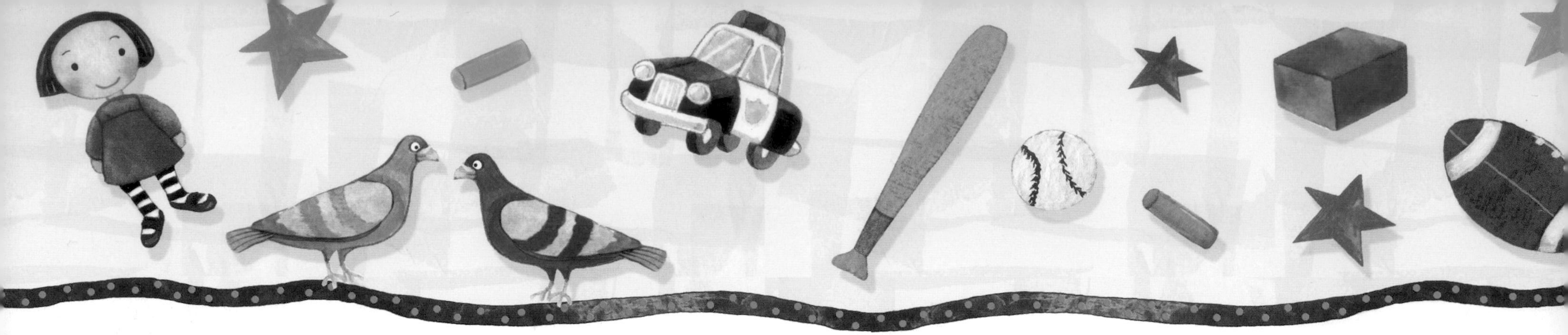

You and I are alike in many ways.

We may be the same age or live on the same street.

We may go to the same school or even have the same name.

STOP

We are different from each other, too.

Our hair may be brown or blond or red or black.

Our eyes may be blue or brown or green.

Our skin may be dark or light or in between.

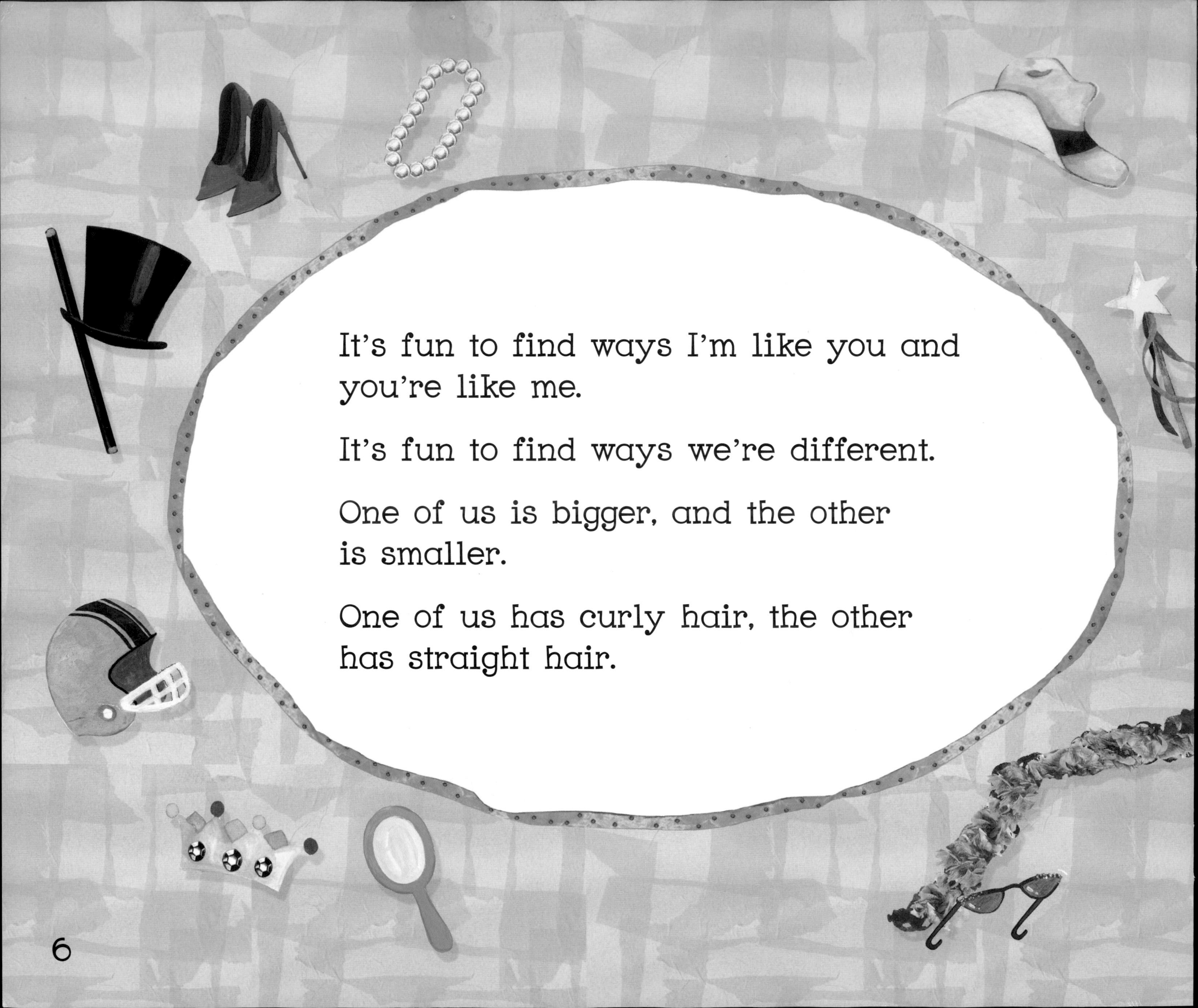

It's fun to find ways I'm like you and you're like me.

It's fun to find ways we're different.

One of us is bigger, and the other is smaller.

One of us has curly hair, the other has straight hair.

I like my body and how I look.

My body is just right for me.

Your body is just right for you.

You're the best!
SPF 30

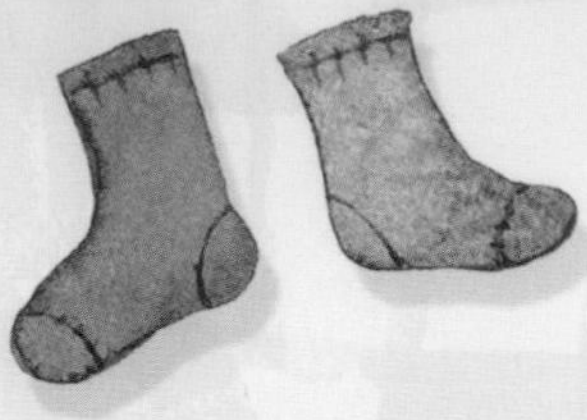

I was a baby once and so were you.

It's fun to look at our baby pictures.

See how little we used to be!

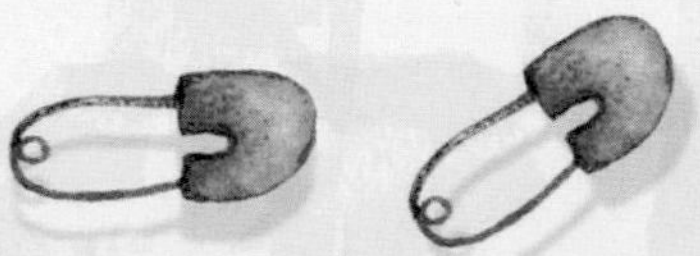
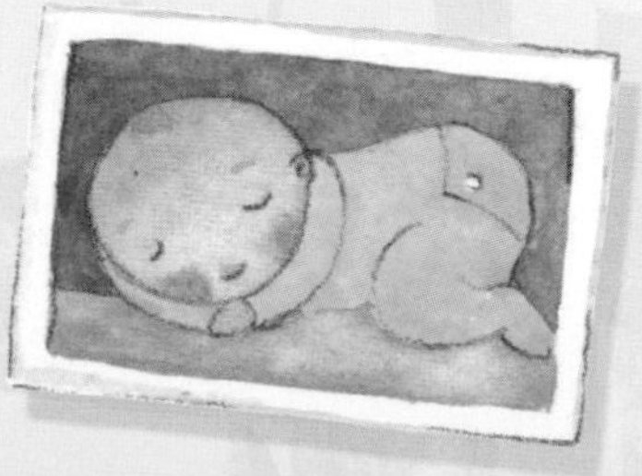

B

I've learned how to do some things by myself, and so have you.

We can both tie our shoes.

We can both ride a bike.

We can both write our names.

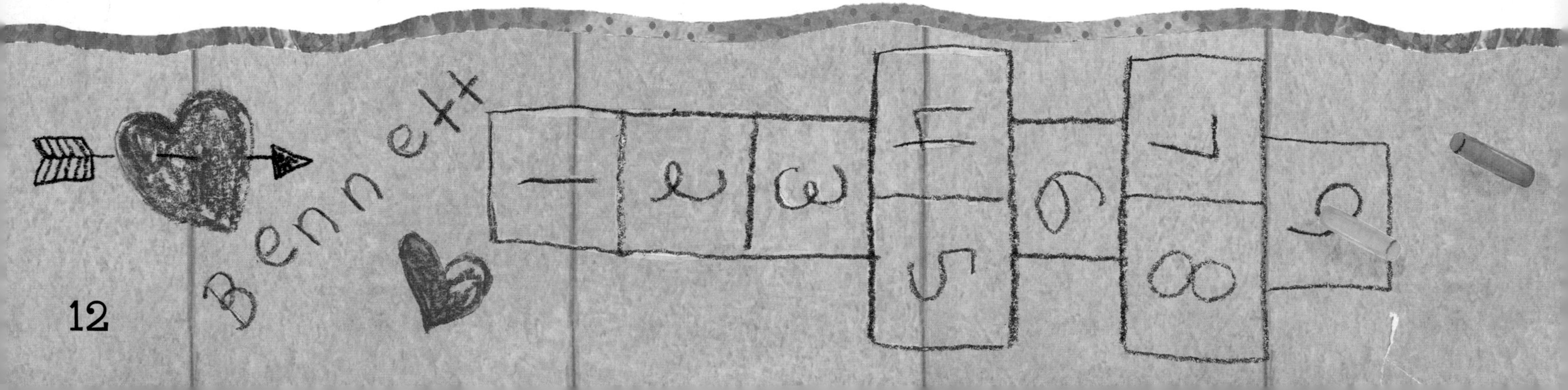

suki

We have different families.

Some families have many people.

Some families have few people.

We celebrate holidays and special days.

Sometimes we celebrate the same holidays.

Sometimes we celebrate different holidays.

Sometimes we celebrate the same holidays
in different ways.

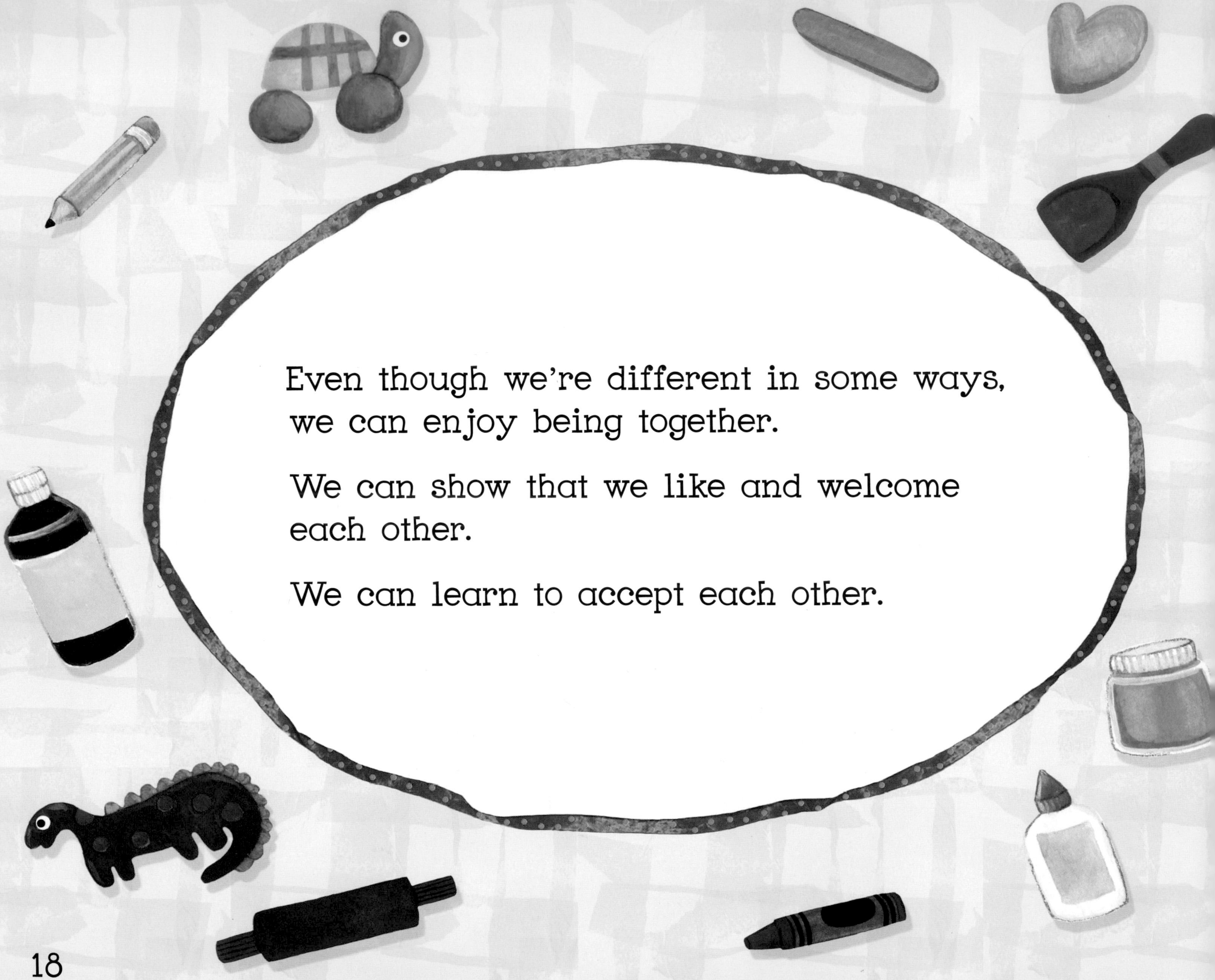

Even though we're different in some ways, we can enjoy being together.

We can show that we like and welcome each other.

We can learn to accept each other.

I feel accepted when you invite me to your home to play.

Or when you want to be my buddy as we line up for playground time.

I feel accepted when you say I'm your friend.

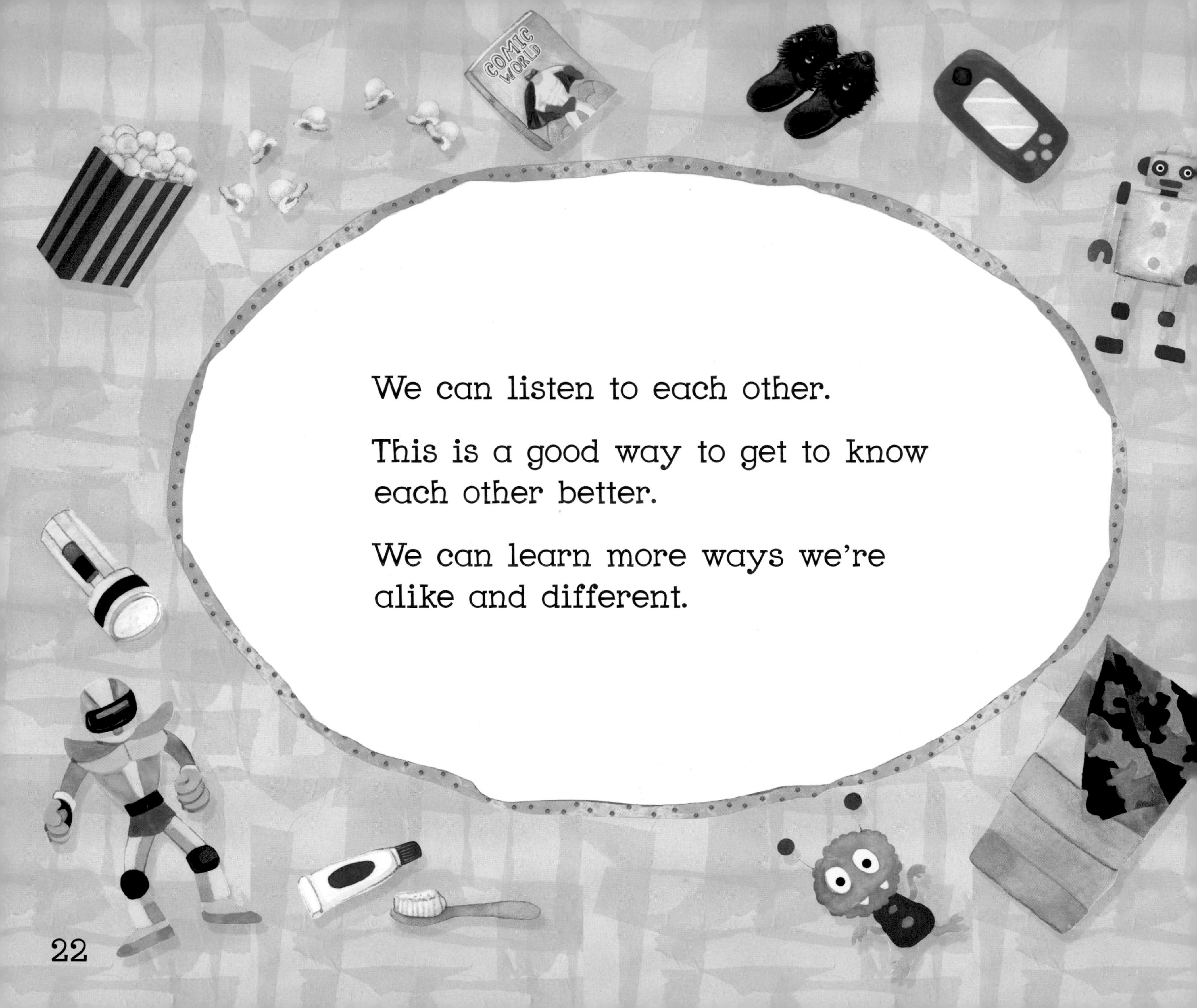

We can listen to each other.

This is a good way to get to know each other better.

We can learn more ways we're alike and different.

AWESOME!

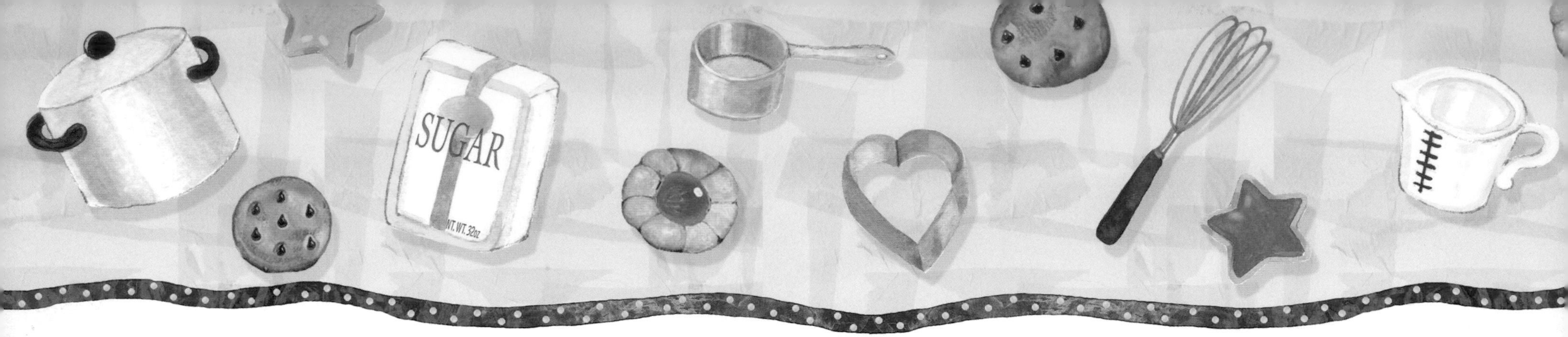

You listen when I tell you a story.

I listen to your stories, too.

I listen when you tell me about something important that happened to you.

Flour
NT. WT. 32oz

We can tell each other about things we like and things we don't like.

We can try our best to understand each other.

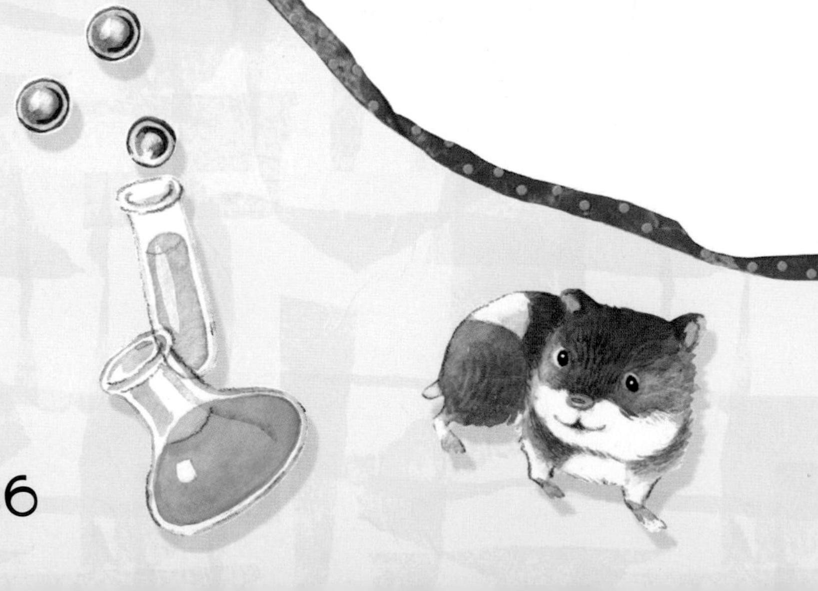

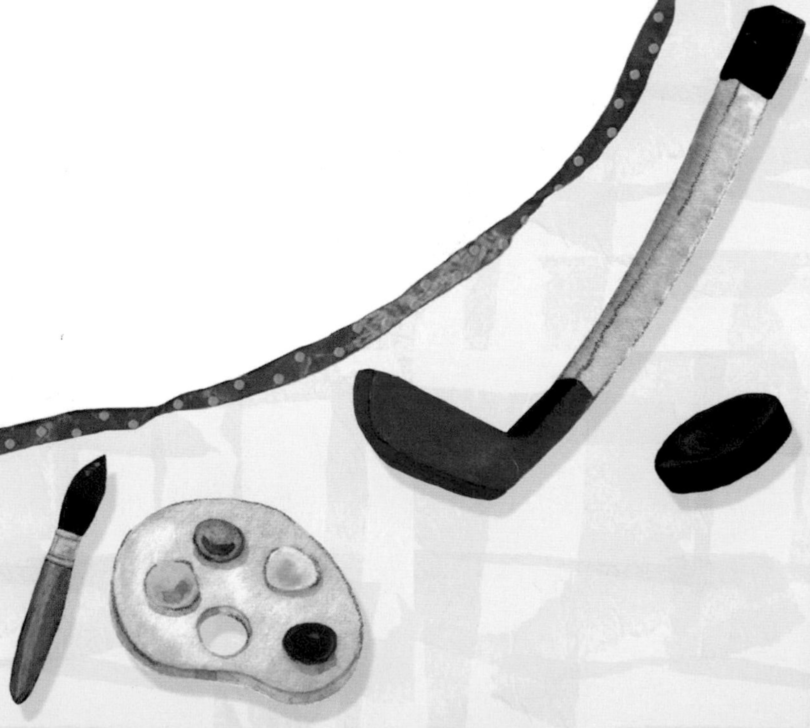

Dinosaurs
SCIENCE TODAY

I can tell you how I'm feeling.

You can tell me how you're feeling, too.

We can tell each other what we want
and what we need.

Sometimes we want the same things.

Sometimes we want different things.

We can try our best to be kind to each other.

Even when we don't agree with each other.

Even when we feel tired or upset.

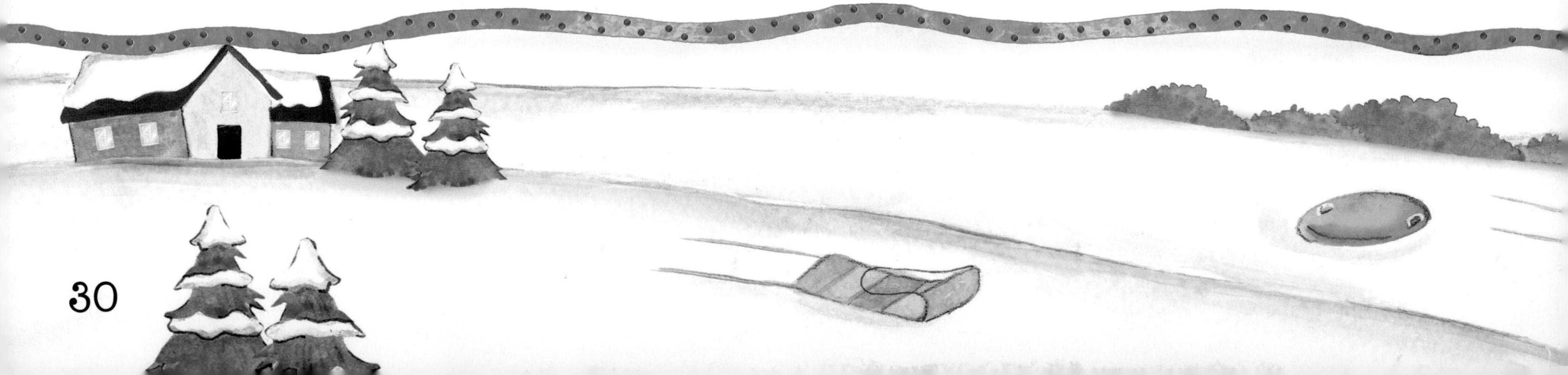

It's unkind to make fun of each other
or call each other names.

That hurts people's feelings.

Let's be nice instead.

We're nice to each other when we hold hands.

When we say "Please" and "Thank you."

When we take turns.

When we give each other help.

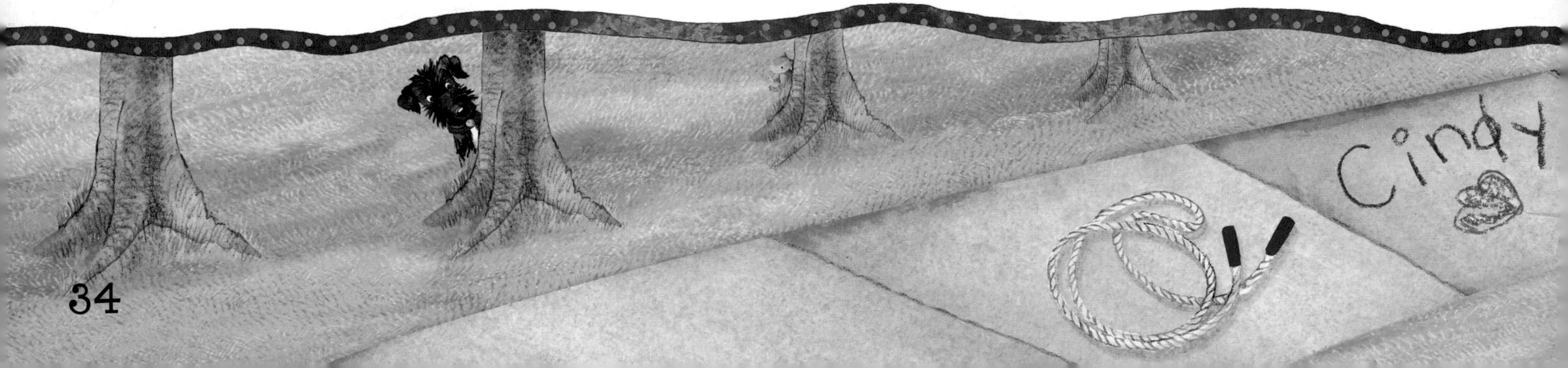

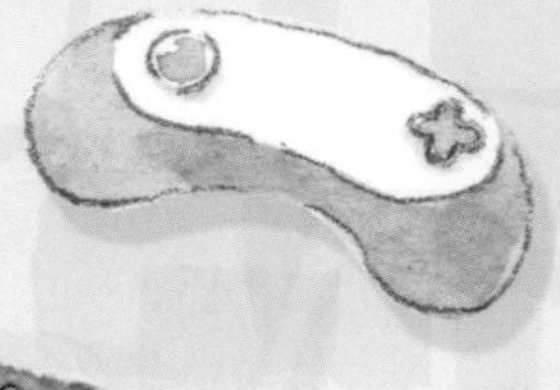

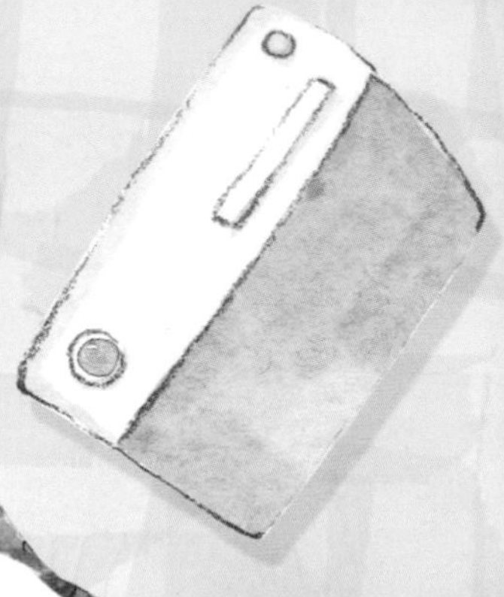

Sometimes we work together
to get things done.

We cooperate with each other.

We cooperate when we build
a sand castle together.

We cooperate when we play a game
all the way to the end, without fighting.

WOW
VIDEO GAME

When we cooperate, we can do almost anything!
We can play together and work together.
We can be friends.

COMMUNITY
GARDEN
CARROT
SEEDS
TOMATO
SEEDS
CARROT
SEEDS

I'm like you, you're like me.

But we're not exactly the same.

That's why I like you and you like me.

Talking with Children About Tolerance and Respect for Others

I'm Like You, You're Like Me addresses the subject of diversity through six concepts: comparing, acceptance, listening, understanding, kindness, and cooperation. These concepts are presented sequentially in the book. As you read, ask children what is happening in the pictures: What are the characters doing? What do you think they are feeling? Be open to children's contributions to the discussion and different interpretations of the concepts. Ask questions that invite children to explain what they are thinking. Acknowledge all responses from children and look for ways to tie their responses into the discussion.

Comparing (pages 2–17)

Making comparisons, in a favorable way, can help children find qualities and interests they share and learn that differences are something to appreciate.

- Compare the characters in the book. How are they alike and different?
- Ask children: How are you and your friends and family members alike and different?

Acceptance (pages 18–21)

As young children develop friendships, they explore the importance of respecting and accepting others. Sharing and taking turns provide opportunities for children to practice acceptance with each other. Ask children:

- Do you think these children are friends? How can you tell?
- What do friends do together? What are some things that you share with friends?

Play simple board games and outdoor games such as ring around the rosy, hopscotch, or tag, and help the children take turns.

Listening (pages 22–25)

Hearing about another person's experiences can spark children's interest and curiosity. Listening reinforces and broadens children's understanding of what people can have in common. Ask kids:

- How can you tell that the children are listening in the picture?

Ask a child to read or tell a story to you or the group. Talk about ways to be a good listener: look at the person who is speaking, listen carefully, and don't interrupt. Ask questions if you have them.

Understanding of Self and Others (pages 26–29)

Children can experience their own uniqueness and that of others by making choices. Provide children opportunities to make choices often throughout the day. Looking at page 27, ask them:

- What kinds of books are these children looking at? What's different about each child's choice?
- What kind of books do you like?

Help children understand how to show and talk about feelings in ways that don't hurt others. Point to different children on page 29 and ask:

- How do you think this child is feeling?
- What do you think this child is saying or feeling?

Model empathic phrases such as, "I understand that you like the rain but are afraid of thunder."

Kindness (pages 30–35)

Teach children how to express kindness through their words and actions. Children can feel empowered by participating in kind acts that provide help to others. Ask:

- How do you think each child in the picture feels? Why?
- Can you tell about a time you helped someone?

Talk about words and actions that are kind. Provide opportunities for children to help, such as putting away games and books, feeding a pet, or cleaning up after a snack.

Cooperation (pages 36–40)

Part of cooperating is being patient. To help kids learn to be patient with each other, give them fun projects with clear goals, such as building a block tower, planting a garden, or doing an art project together. Ask:

- Do you think the children in this picture are having a good time? Why?
- What are some things you and your friends do together? How do you make sure you get along?
- How do you think it feels when people work hard together and finish a job?

Model understanding, acceptance, and all the concepts outlined in this book. Children need to feel accepted, valued, and understood in order to learn to accept, value, and understand others.

About the Author

Over her 28-year career, Cindy Gainer has worked with and for children in many capacities, including as an educator, proprietor of a preschool, athletic mentor, award-winning author, illustrator, musician, workshop presenter, and support professional for children with special needs.

Cindy resides near Pittsburgh, Pennsylvania, with her husband, Bill, and son, August.

About the Illustrator

Miki Sakamoto's interest in illustration began during her childhood as she sketched, colored, and painted away for hours in her room. Her artwork is inspired by all her nieces and nephews. Miki resides in Orange County, California, with her husband Kevin, her cat Jake, and mouse Millie. She has illustrated several picture books, including *What I Like About Me* by Allia Zobel Nolan and *My First Garden* by Wendy Lewison.

Join the Free Spirit Advisory Board

Teachers, Administrators, Librarians, Counselors, Youth Workers, and **Social Workers,** help us create the resources you need to support the kids you serve. In order to make our books and other products even more beneficial for children and teens, the Free Spirit Advisory Board provides valuable feedback on content, art, title concepts, and more. For more information, go to **www.freespirit.com/Advisory-Boards**.

More Great Products from Free Spirit

F Is for Feelings

by Goldie Millar and Lisa Berger, illustrated by Hazel Mitchell

We all feel many different emotions every day. This friendly and positive alphabet book gives children those "feelings words," and explores the idea that while some feelings are more comfortable than others, all are natural and important. Ages 3–8.

40 pp., color illust., PB & HC, 11¼" x 9¼".

I Like Being Me

Poems about kindness, friendship, and making good choices

by Judy Lalli, M.S.

Twenty-five short rhyming poems invite children to believe in themselves, learn from mistakes, cooperate, share, help others, solve problems, be kind, tell the truth, make positive choices, and more. This charming update to a popular volume of poetry is perfect for teaching social skills to young children. Ages 4–8.

64 pp., B&W photos, color illust., PB, 8" x 8".

Just Because I Am

A Child's Book of Affirmation

by Lauren Murphy Payne, MSW, LCSW, illustrated by Melissa Iwai

Young children need support and encouragement as they learn to value themselves. This book of sweet, simple affirmations for children builds self-esteem and self-confidence through clear language and colorful art. *Just Because I Am* invites little ones to love, accept, and feel good about themselves exactly as they are. Ages 4–8.

36 pp., color illust., PB & HC, 11¼" x 9¼".

We Can Get Along

A Child's Book of Choices

by Lauren Murphy Payne, MSW, LCSW, illustrated by Melissa Iwai

At times, all children need a little help getting along with others and respecting differences. *We Can Get Along* uses clear, affirming words and charming full-color illustrations to teach young children tolerance, kindness, and conflict resolution. Ages 4–8.

40 pp., color illust., PB & HC, 11¼" x 9¼".

Interested in purchasing multiple quantities and receiving volume discounts? Contact edsales@freespirit.com or call 1.800.735.7323 and ask for Education Sales.
Many Free Spirit authors are available for speaking engagements, workshops, and keynotes. Contact speakers@freespirit.com or call 1.800.735.7323.

For pricing information, to place an order, or to request a free catalog, contact:

Free Spirit Publishing Inc. • 6325 Sandburg Road • Suite 100 • Minneapolis, MN 55427-3674 • toll-free 800.735.7323
local 612.338.2068 • fax 612.337.5050 • help4kids@freespirit.com • www.freespirit.com

Free Spirit's Learning to Get Along® Series

Help children learn, understand, and practice basic social and emotional skills. Real-life situations, diversity, and concrete examples make these read-aloud books appropriate for childcare settings, schools, and the home. *Each book: 40 pp., color illust., PB, 9" x 9", ages 4–8.*

ACCEPT AND VALUE EACH PERSON
Introduces diversity and related concepts: respecting differences, being inclusive, and appreciating people just the way they are.

BE CAREFUL AND STAY SAFE
Teaches children how to avoid potential dangers, ask for help, follow directions, use things carefully, and plan ahead.

BE HONEST AND TELL THE TRUTH
Children learn that being honest in words and actions builds self-confidence and trust, and that telling the truth can take courage and tact.

BE POLITE AND KIND
Introduces children to good manners and gracious behavior including saying "Please," "Thank you," "Excuse me," and "I'm sorry."

COOL DOWN AND WORK THROUGH ANGER
Teaches skills for working through anger: self-calming, getting help, talking and listening, apologizing, and viewing others positively.

JOIN IN AND PLAY
Teaches the basics of cooperation, getting along, making friends, and being a friend.

KNOW AND FOLLOW RULES
Shows children that following rules can help us stay safe, learn, be fair, get along, and instill a positive sense of pride.

LISTEN AND LEARN
Introduces and explains what listening means, why it's important to listen, and how to listen well.

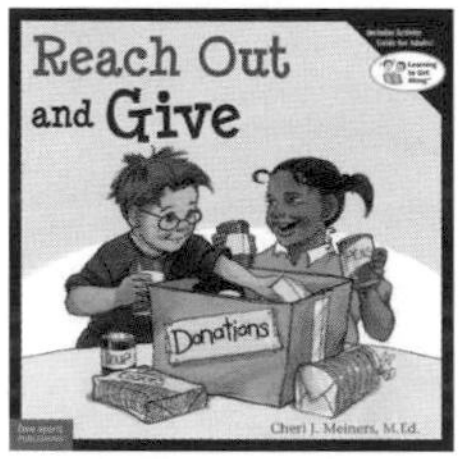

REACH OUT AND GIVE
Begins with the concept of gratitude; shows children contributing to their community in simple yet meaningful ways.

RESPECT AND TAKE CARE OF THINGS
Children learn to put things where they belong and ask permission to use things. Teaches simple environmental awareness.

SHARE AND TAKE TURNS
Gives reasons to share; describes four ways to share; points out that children can also share their knowledge, creativity, and time.

TALK AND WORK IT OUT
Peaceful conflict resolution is simplified so children can learn to calm down, state the problem, listen, and think of and try solutions.

TRY AND STICK WITH IT
Introduces children to flexibility, stick-to-it-iveness (perseverance), and the benefits of trying something new.

UNDERSTAND AND CARE
Builds empathy in children; guides them to show they care by listening to others and respecting their feelings.

WHEN I FEEL AFRAID
Helps children understand their fears; teaches simple coping skills; encourages children to talk with trusted adults about their fears.

LEARNING TO GET ALONG® SERIES INTERACTIVE SOFTWARE
Children follow along or read on their own, using a special highlight feature to click or hear word definitions. User's Guide included. *For Mac and Windows.*

www.freespirit.com • 800.735.7323

Volume discounts: edsales@freespirit.com
Speakers bureau: speakers@freespirit.com